★ IT'S MY STATE! ★

SOUTH CAROLINA

Debra Hess

William McGeveran

Marshall Cavendish
Benchmark
New York

Published by Marshall Cavendish Benchmark
An imprint of Marshall Cavendish Corporation

Website: www.marshallcavendish.us

Other Marshall Cavendish Offices:
Marshall Cavendish International (Asia) Private Limited, 1 New Industrial Road, Singapore 536196 •
Marshall Cavendish International (Thailand) Co Ltd. 253 Asoke, 12th Flr, Sukhumvit 21 Road, Klongtoey Nua,
Wattana, Bangkok 10110, Thailand • Marshall Cavendish (Malaysia) Sdn Bhd, Times Subang, Lot 46, Subang
Hi-Tech Industrial Park, Batu Tiga, 40000 Shah Alam, Selangor Darul Ehsan, Malaysia

Marshall Cavendish is a trademark of Times Publishing Limited

All websites were available and accurate when this book was sent to press.

Library of Congress Cataloging-in-Publication Data
Hess, Debra.
          South Carolina / Debra Hess and William McGeveran.—2nd ed.
              p. cm. — (It's my state!)
          Summary: "Surveys the history, geography, government, economy, and people
          of South Carolina"—Provided by publisher.
          Includes bibliographical references and index.
          ISBN 978-1-60870-526-9 (print) — ISBN 978-1-60870-704-1 (ebook)
          1. South Carolina--Juvenile literature. I. McGeveran, William. II. Title.
      F269.3.H47 2012
      975.7—dc22   2010044336

Second Edition developed for Marshall Cavendish Benchmark by RJF Publishing LLC (www.RJFpublishing.com)
Series Designer, Second Edition: Tammy West/Westgraphix LLC
Editor, Second Edition: Emily Dolbear

CONTENTS

State Tree: Palmetto

The palmetto tree, also called the sabal palm or the cabbage palmetto, has a spongy trunk and large fanlike leaves that can grow longer than 7 feet (2 meters). The palmetto played a role in the American Revolution because a fort made from its wood repelled British cannonballs.

State Flower: Yellow Jessamine

Yellow jessamine vines wrap around trees and fences all over the state. The leaves are green throughout the year, and the bright yellow, trumpet-shaped flowers bloom in early spring. The flowers are both pretty and poisonous.

State Bird: Carolina Wren

The Carolina wren can be found in woods, fields, or swamps. It may build its nest in odd places—even in boxes, flowerpots, or shoes. A wren couple stays together for life. This bird, along with the palmetto and the yellow jessamine, appears on the South Carolina quarter that was issued by the U.S. Mint in 2000.

State Animal: White-tailed Deer

White-tailed deer are often seen in the South Carolina woods. They can run up to 30 miles (50 kilometers) an hour. When the deer is alarmed, it may lift up its tail, showing a white underside. This is a warning to nearby deer to be on their guard.

State Reptile: Loggerhead Sea Turtle

At the suggestion of a fifth-grade class, these big turtles were named as the official state reptile in 1988. The adults weigh around 250 pounds (100 kilograms). Every year, the females lay their eggs on beaches. Unfortunately, few loggerheads survive to adulthood. Because their population is threatened—likely to become endangered, or at risk of dying out—programs have been set up to help protect them.

State Dog: Boykin Spaniel

A South Carolina hunter named Whit Boykin bred the first Boykin spaniels a hundred years ago. People still use Boykin spaniels to hunt many kinds of game. These dogs also make excellent family pets.

★1★ The Palmetto State

One of the thirteen original colonies that formed the United States, South Carolina is located in the southeastern United States, along the Atlantic coast. It stretches some 275 miles (440 km) from the mountains and hills in the west to the seacoast, with its sandy beaches, in the east. It extends some 220 miles (350 km) from north to south.

South Carolina is not a big state. With a land area of 30,110 square miles (77,983 square kilometers), it is the tenth-smallest U.S. state and the smallest state in the Deep South. In population, South Carolina ranks twenty-fourth, or around the middle. It is divided into forty-six counties. The biggest county by area is Horry County, along the coast to the north. This county includes the resort area of Myrtle Beach.

Despite its size, South Carolina stands out in many ways. Spanish explorers first came to the region in the sixteenth century, and the English settled Charleston, one of the South's oldest and most beautiful cities, in 1670. In 1788, South Carolina became the eighth state to ratify (approve) the U.S. Constitution. A stronghold of cotton plantations and slavery, South Carolina

Quick Facts

SOUTH CAROLINA BORDERS

North	North Carolina
South	Georgia
	Atlantic Ocean
East	Atlantic Ocean
West	Georgia

South Carolina Counties

GREENVILLE · CHEROKEE · YORK · PICKENS · SPARTANBURG · OCONEE · LANCASTER · MARLBORO · CHESTER · CHESTERFILED · UNION · ANDERSON · LAURENS · FAIRFIELD · DARLINGTON · DILLON · ABBEVILLE · NEWBERRY · KERSHAW · LEE · FLORENCE · MARION · GREENWOOD · SALUDA · RICHLAND · MCCORMICK · LEXINGTON · SUMTER · HORRY · EDGEFIELD · CALHOUN · CLARENDON · WILLIAMSBURG · AIKEN · ORANGEBURG · GEORGETOWN · BARNWELL · BAMBERG · DORCHESTER · BERKELEY · ALLENDALE · COLLETON · HAMPTON · CHARLESTON · JASPER · BEAUFORT

South Carolina has 46 counties.

seceded (withdrew) from the United States in December 1860, becoming the first state to do so. The Civil War broke out when its troops fired on Fort Sumter, in Charleston Harbor, in April 1861.

The civil rights movement helped improve race relations in the state during the 1950s and afterward. Today, the population is growing, and tourism is among many industries adding to the diverse economy. South Carolinians and visitors alike enjoy the state's mild climate and historic and cultural attractions, as well as its forests, parks, gardens, beaches, and golf courses.

The Landscape

South Carolina can be divided into three geographic regions. They cross the state diagonally in three belts of varying size. The Blue Ridge region occupies the northwest corner, along the border with Georgia and North Carolina. It is the smallest of the three regions. Below it, to the south and east, is a large hilly region known as the Piedmont. These two belts make up what South Carolinians call the "upcountry." South and east of the Piedmont is the Atlantic Coastal Plain, which covers around two-thirds of the state. This region is often called the "lowcountry."

The Blue Ridge Region

The northwest corner of the state is covered by the Blue Ridge Mountains, which stretch from northern Georgia to southern Pennsylvania. They are part of the larger Appalachian mountain system, which runs through much of the eastern

The Blue Ridge Mountains, in the state's far northwest corner, get their name from their beautiful bluish color when seen from afar.

part of the United States. Sassafras Mountain, within the Blue Ridge Mountains, rises 3,560 feet (1,085 m) above sea level. This is the state's highest point.

The Blue Ridge region is a scenic area with dense forests and winding streams. A portion of the Sumter National Forest is located there, along with a number of state parks. There are excellent hiking trails, as well as lakes and rivers ideal for boating or fishing. The Chattooga River, which runs along South Carolina's northwestern border, is popular with white-water rafters.

The Piedmont

The land in between the Blue Ridge Mountains and the Atlantic Coastal Plain is called the Piedmont. This region is part of a long line of rolling hills that stretches from New York to Alabama. In South Carolina, the hills of the Piedmont can measure from around 200 feet (60 m) to more than 1,000 feet (300 m) above sea level. The Piedmont also has forests, lakes, and fast-flowing rivers and streams.

The Atlantic Coastal Plain

Over millions of years, as sea levels rose and fell, ocean currents

Many waterfalls flow down the Blue Ridge Mountains.

Hilton Head Island is a luxurious resort area along the coast to the south of the state.

created a wide plain along the state's Atlantic coast. Several of South Carolina's largest cities are located in this region.

More than 60 miles (about 100 km) of the coastline in the north is made up of white, sandy beaches, the so-called Grand Strand. The Sea Islands extend along much of the state's Atlantic coast, and down into Georgia and north Florida. They are separated from the mainland by saltwater marshes and estuaries. Hilton Head Island, near the southern tip of the state, is the best known of these islands and a popular vacation spot.

On South Carolina's mainland, and to the west of the coastline, is a stretch of forests called the Pine Barrens. They are home to a wide variety of wildlife. The Sand Hills, to the west of the Pine Barrens, rise as high as 600 feet (180 m). The state capital, Columbia, lies in these hills.

Waterways

Thousands of years ago, the Atlantic Coastal Plain in South Carolina was covered with water. As the waters gradually receded, swamps, marshes, and small lakes remained. The state's large lakes are artificial. The biggest lake in South Carolina is Lake Marion. It was created by a dam built on the Santee River in the early 1940s. Lake Marion has an area of 173 square miles (448 sq km) and covers parts of five counties.

South Carolina is actually drained by three major river systems that empty into the Atlantic Ocean. They are the Santee, the Savannah, and the Pee Dee. Around the middle of the state is the Santee, which flows southeast into the Atlantic Ocean after 143 miles (230 km). The Santee and its tributaries are South Carolina's most important river system. To the south along the border with Georgia is the Savannah River. It stretches 314 miles (505 km) to the ocean near Savannah, Georgia. In the north is the Pee Dee, which empties into Winyah Bay near Georgetown. For years, South Carolinians have used the power of all this flowing water to produce usable energy called hydroelectric power.

Quick Facts

A PLANNED CITY
In 1786, lawmakers agreed to create a new capital city near the center of the state to replace Charleston. Columbia was the second planned city in the United States—the first was New Haven, Connecticut. Planners divided the city into four hundred blocks, with half-acre (0.2-hectare) lots and wide streets. By 1800, it had close to a thousand residents. Today, Columbia is the state's biggest city, with a population of about 130,000.

The modern Arthur Ravenel Jr. Bridge, also called the Cooper River Bridge, spans the tidal Cooper River in Charleston. It was built to withstand strong winds.

Climate

The Atlantic Coast is the warmest part of the state, and the mountains in the northwest are the coldest. Average January temperatures in Charleston range from around 38 degrees Fahrenheit (3 degrees Celsius) to 60 °F (16 °C), while they range from around 30 °F (−1 °C) to 50 °F (10 °C) in the Blue Ridge Mountains. These mountains are often covered with snow, but winters in the rest of South Carolina are generally mild. In most of the state, it is unusual to get more than a dusting of snow.

During the summer, the weather often gets hot and muggy. Temperatures in the lowcountry may even soar above 100 °F (38 °C). Ocean breezes and cool water along the coast help to make the heat more tolerable. Rainfall in the state is considerable. In the Blue Ridge Mountains, more than 70 inches (178 centimeters) of rain fall each year. The entire state's average rainfall is about 50 inches (127 cm).

South Carolinians seldom have to deal with heavy snowstorms, but tropical storms hit the state from time to time. One of the worst was the Sea Islands hurricane of August 1893. More than one thousand people were killed, mostly by drowning, in Georgia and South Carolina. Some 30,000 people were left homeless. More recently, in September 1989, Hurricane Hugo destroyed homes,

With its ideal climate and landscape, the Myrtle Beach area calls itself the Golf Capital of the World.

Hurricane Hugo ripped apart many houses in South Carolina in 1989.

In Their Own Words

People were to be seen flying from tottering houses, and with trees falling . . . and boards and shingles and tin flying in every direction, the scene was one never to be forgotten.

—S. H. Rodgers, editor of the Beaufort *Palmetto Post*, of the 1893 Sea Islands storm

knocked down trees, and caused billions of dollars in damage in the Sea Islands and elsewhere in the lowcountry. The storm killed thirty-five people in South Carolina.

Wildlife

About two-thirds of the land in South Carolina is still made up of woods. There are four state forests and four national forest areas, and there is forestland in the forty-seven state parks. On the Coastal Plain, there are oak, red maple,

Caesars Head State Park, near the North Carolina border, offers beautiful views and unspoiled woodland trails.

hickory, and cypress trees, and palmetto trees are a familiar sight near the shore. Oak and hemlock trees grow in the Blue Ridge Mountains. Hickories, oaks, and dogwoods can be found in the Piedmont. Forests of cypress, sweet gum, and other trees grow in wet areas. Pine trees of many varieties can be found all over South Carolina.

A wide variety of native plants grow wild in South Carolina and, in many cases, also grow in gardens. The mountainous areas are especially known for their colorful azaleas, rhododendrons, and mountain laurel. Swamps and river bottoms feature plants such as honeysuckle, Venus flytrap, and yellow jessamine, the widely grown state flower.

Quick Facts

BEARS ON THE MOVE

Black bears still roam the woods in parts of South Carolina. As more people build homes in their range, black bears even show up in backyards. Experts say that, in areas where there are bears, it is important not to leave food or garbage around outside houses or in campgrounds. These things may attract bears, and although black bears do not often attack humans, they are powerful wild animals.

A cottonmouth water moccasin looks for prey in South Carolina's Francis Beidler Forest.

South Carolina's forests and hills are home to many animals. Herds of white-tailed deer, the state animal, range freely through the countryside. South Carolina also has bears, bobcats, opossums, raccoons, squirrels, foxes, and cottontail rabbits. Birds such as wrens, orioles, catbirds, hawks, and eagles fly through South Carolina skies and nest in the trees and thickets.

Waterfowl such as ducks, geese, and swans swim across the state's lakes and ponds. Egrets and herons live in the swamps. Trout, carp, catfish, and striped bass, the state fish, are common freshwater fish. In the coastal waters are sharks, dolphins, giant turtles, and an occasional sperm whale as well as oysters, crabs, and clams. The swamps and marshes have alligators and many species of frogs and snakes, including poisonous water moccasins and copperheads.

Pollution, overhunting or overfishing, and loss of habitat have harmed some types of animals. Dozens of South Carolina's animal and plant species are listed as threatened or endangered. Among the endangered animals are the Indiana bat, the red-cockaded woodpecker, and a mussel called the Carolina heelsplitter. Laws limit or prohibit hunting or fishing for certain species, and breeding programs have been set up to help increase certain animal populations.

A red-cockaded woodpecker searches for insects on the trunk of a pine tree. These birds are endangered in part because of loss of habitat.

Eastern Tiger Swallowtail Butterfly

South Carolina's official butterfly is the Eastern tiger swallowtail. The adult male has yellow and black wings. The female's wings can be either yellow or bluish black. These butterflies use their long tubelike tongues to suck nectar from flowers.

American Alligator

These alligators live in the swamps and waters of the Coastal Plain. They like to bask in the sun and can live for more than sixty years. They are no longer endangered, but they are listed as a threatened species, partly because of habitat loss and pollutants in the water.

Sassafras

Most sassafras trees grow in moist and sandy soils. The tree has a distinctive smell that many people find pleasing. In the past, American Indians used the leaf, bark, and root of the sassafras to make medicine and to flavor food.

Spotted Salamander

This amphibian is known for its dark-colored body dotted with bright spots of color. Spotted salamanders spend much of their lives underground in the woods. When they feel threatened, their skin releases a white sticky liquid that poisons their attackers.

Kudzu

Sometimes called "The Vine That Ate the South," kudzu was brought to the American South from Japan to adorn gardens in the 1870s. It can sometimes grow as fast as 1 foot (30 cm) a day during the summer months, wrapping around trees and almost anything else in its path. Today, this thick leafy vine is considered a weed.

Striped Bass

The striped bass is the state fish of South Carolina. Sport fishers prize the size and fighting spirit of the striped bass. Some striped bass may weigh 30 to 40 pounds (14 to 18 kg).

From the Beginning

Archaeologists digging near the Savannah River, in an area now part of South Carolina, have found evidence that people may have been living in the region as far back as 16,000 years ago or more, during the last Ice Age. These tribes hunted, fished, and gathered nuts and berries. Stone spear points that they made can still be found in the hills of South Carolina. Ancient tribes probably moved from place to place, looking for available food. Eventually, they learned to farm the land. They settled in villages and planted crops of beans, squash, and maize (corn). Women commonly did most of the farming, while men hunted and, when necessary, fought enemies. In time, the early inhabitants of the region also learned to make pottery from clay. Pieces of Indian pottery can be found today in parts of the state.

By the sixteenth century, Cherokee Indians were living in the northwestern

Quick Facts

INDIAN SLAVES

South Carolina was once a center of the Indian slave trade. American Indians captured there were exported to other colonies in North America and the Caribbean or sold within the colony. Around the beginning of the eighteenth century, about one-third of the slaves in South Carolina were Indians. As the Indian population declined, plantation owners bought more and more black slaves.

Fort Sumter in Charleston Harbor played a key role in the history of South Carolina and of the nation. Today, the fort is part of a national monument.

Carolina colonists flee in canoes from attack by American Indians.

part of present-day South Carolina. Other groups living in the area included the Edistoes, Waterees, and Keowees. By the end of the seventeenth century, the Yamassee and Catawba tribes had also settled there.

Some 15,000 to 30,000 American Indians may have lived in the region when European explorers arrived in the sixteenth century. The Indians lacked immunity to the diseases carried by the Europeans. As a result, many thousands died from diseases such as smallpox, influenza, and measles. Others died in battle or were taken as slaves. The Indian population was greatly reduced by contact with Europeans, and the Indian way of life was never the same.

The European Settlers

South Carolina eventually became an English colony, but only after both the French and the Spanish had tried to start permanent settlements there. In 1521, a Spanish ship from the colony of Santo Domingo in the Caribbean landed in Winyah Bay on the coast of present-day South Carolina. The Spaniards invited some Indians onto their ship and then set sail for Santo Domingo, taking them as slaves. One of the Indians became a servant to Lucas Vásquez de Ayllón, who had helped pay for the expedition. The servant told wonderful stories about his homeland, which he claimed was a rich land ruled by a giant king.

In the summer of 1526, Ayllón set out for the Carolina coast with about five hundred Spaniards and some black slaves—the first of hundreds of thousands to be brought to the American South. He started a settlement named San Miguel de Gualdape. It was the first European settlement on land that is now part of the United States. But the Spaniards soon discovered that the wonderful stories were untrue, and many Spanish settlers died from hunger and disease. After Ayllón's death, the slaves rebelled against their captors. That winter, surviving settlers tried to return to Europe, though many died during the difficult journey home.

In 1562, a group of Protestants from France set up a small settlement near what is now Port Royal. They had suffered discrimination in France, where most people and the country's rulers were Catholic. The French Protestants wanted to live where they could freely practice their religion. This settlement also failed. As their food and supplies ran out, the colonists tried to sail back to France. Many starved to death on the way.

In 1566, Spain established a settlement called Santa Elena on Port Royal Sound, near present-day Beaufort. It had more than four hundred people by 1575. For a short time, it served as the capital of Spain's La Florida province, which included a large area of the southeastern part of North America.

In 1587, as a result of English attacks on Spanish Florida, Santa Elena was abandoned, and by the early 1600s, England had taken possession of much of the land that is now South Carolina. In 1629, England's King Charles I gave a large tract of land—including present-day North Carolina and South Carolina—as a gift to Sir Robert Heath. He wanted it to be called *Carolana*, which is Latin for "land of Charles." (Later, the spelling was changed to Carolina.) Sir Robert did little to attract settlers, and in 1663, King Charles II, son of Charles I, gave the colony to eight noblemen called Lords Proprietors. They offered land, freedom of religion, and a new way of life to anyone who would travel there.

CITY OF THE OLD SOUTH

Founded in 1670, Charles Towne (known as Charleston from 1783) is one of the oldest cities in the United States. It became a major seaport for trade in deerskins, rice, indigo, and later, cotton. By 1790, Charleston was the fourth-biggest city in the United States—after New York, Philadelphia, and Boston. Its historic district today is notable for its narrow streets, lush gardens, beautiful old homes, and other reminders of its role in the history of the South and of the nation.

In 1670, two shiploads of people landed in the region. Many were from the island of Barbados, which was then under English rule. They started a settlement at Albemarle Point, later moving it a short distance away to Oyster Point. The settlement was known as Charles Towne (present-day Charleston). As it grew, more settlers moved into other parts of the area. Early in the next century, Carolina was divided into North Carolina and South Carolina.

American Indians in South Carolina often cooperated with the newcomers, but the colonists took more and more land for rice fields. English traders also often abused the Indians and took many as slaves. The anger of the Yamassee and other tribes increased. In 1715, their warriors raced up the coast of South Carolina, burning homes and killing settlers as they went. It was the start of the Yamassee War. Many settlers fled to Charles Towne, but before long, the Yamassee and their allies were defeated.

Another threat to the colonists were the pirates who sailed up and down the coast. They docked their ships at ports and raided the cities. The many islands off the coast made it easy for them to hide their ships and treasures. Among these pirates was Edward Teach, better known as Blackbeard.

In addition to these dangers, the English settlers in South Carolina also feared that Spain or France would try to take over the territory. Partly because the Lords Proprietors refused to provide money for the colony's defense, the settlers rebelled against them and asked King George I for help. He eventually took control of the colony, and it was ruled directly by the British monarch through an appointed royal governor.

Edward Teach, or Blackbeard, and his crew robbed merchant ships along the Carolina coast.

Revolution and Statehood

By the mid–1700s, many people in South Carolina and other colonies were unhappy with the British government. They wanted to change Britain's tax and trade rules and to have more of a voice in government. In September 1774, leaders from South Carolina and other American colonies met in Philadelphia for the First Continental Congress. They

Nathanael Greene served as a commander of the Continental Army in the South during the American Revolution.

decided not to allow any goods to be imported from Britain and sent a list of grievances to the British king, George III. These grievances were ignored.

By April 1775, colonists in New England were fighting against the British army—in effect, the American Revolution had begun. In July 1776, representatives from all thirteen colonies voted to declare independence. Supporters of independence were called Patriots. Other colonists, known as Loyalists, sided with the British.

A small British force had already bombarded the harbor of Charles Towne, but they were beaten back at Sullivan's Island in June 1776. Two years later, the British began an assault on the South. They gained control of Georgia, and in May 1780, captured Charles Towne. A few months later, British troops crushed Patriot forces and units of the colonists' Continental Army in the Battle of Camden.

But the Patriots never gave up. Well over a hundred battles were fought in South Carolina—more than in any other state. Forces under General Nathanael Greene and Patriot leader Francis Marion harassed and defeated British troops and their allies all over the region.

In Their Own Words

Our band is few but true and tried,
Our leader frank and bold;
The British soldier trembles
When Marion's name is told.

—American poet William Cullen Bryant (1794–1878), "Song of Marion"

At the Battle of Kings Mountain in 1780, a band of Patriot farmers scored a quick, decisive victory over Loyalist forces.

At the Battle of Kings Mountain in 1780, some nine hundred Patriot farmers from the Blue Ridge Mountains banded together. In about one hour, they defeated a regiment of more than a thousand Loyalist soldiers.

The main British army in the South surrendered after a crushing defeat at Yorktown, Virginia, in October 1781. With the signing of a peace treaty two years later, officially ending the war, the colonies were free of British rule. On May 23, 1788, South Carolina ratified the new U.S. Constitution and became the eighth state of the Union (another term for the United States).

Slavery and the Road to the Civil War

From South Carolina's earliest days as a colony, farmers used slaves to work in the fields. Most were black people brought to the American mainland either directly from Africa or via the islands in the Caribbean. As demand for export crops such as rice and indigo increased, more and more black slaves were brought to South Carolina. By the early 1700s, the number of slaves outnumbered the number of white people.

In 1793, the cotton gin was invented, providing an easier way to remove the seeds from cotton. Soon after, machines were developed to manufacture cloth on a large scale. Cotton was now in heavy demand and became South Carolina's biggest cash crop and export. Cotton plantations grew and prospered, built on slave labor. Because of the large slave population, the colony's plantation owners, or planters, were always afraid of a major revolt. By the early 1800s, they also began to fear that the federal government could act to abolish (end) slavery.

Slave labor on cotton plantations enriched South Carolina in the years before the Civil War.

Many South Carolinians were also concerned about tariffs, which are taxes on products traded between countries. In 1828, the federal government imposed high tariffs on manufactured goods imported from abroad. (A tariff helps protect a country's own products by making imports more expensive to buy.) The 1828 tariff helped industrial states, but it did not help South Carolina, which mostly produced crops like cotton. In fact, it meant that planters in the South had to pay much higher prices for manufactured goods.

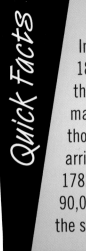
The Magnolia Plantation was built on the Ashley River in Charleston in 1679. It is one of the South's oldest plantations.

South Carolina's leaders called a state convention and declared that the federal laws establishing the tariff of 1828, and a later one in 1832, violated the rights of states under the U.S. Constitution. They claimed that a state had the right to declare any such federal law null and void. (This asserted right became known as the principle of "nullification.") They threatened that South Carolina would secede from the Union if the federal government tried to collect these tariffs in their state.

President Andrew Jackson got Congress to pass a measure allowing him to use the army and navy, if necessary, to enforce federal law in South Carolina. But he also worked out a compromise that reduced the tariffs. South Carolina's leaders agreed, and the threat of secession was removed for a while.

However, South Carolina's leaders believed that the future of slavery would be in danger if Abraham Lincoln was elected president. In December 1860, a month after Lincoln was elected, South Carolina seceded from the United States.

In Their Own Words

We, the people of the State of South Carolina, in Convention assembled, do declare and ordain . . . that the union now subsisting between South Carolina and the other states, under the name of the United States of America is hereby dissolved.

—Ordinance of Secession, December 20, 1860

Over the next several months, ten other Southern states also seceded, and all eleven joined together to form the Confederate States of America. President Lincoln did not accept the right of states to secede from the Union. He was determined to keep the Union from breaking up.

The Civil War

The Civil War began in earnest in April 1861, when the Union commander refused to surrender Fort Sumter in the harbor of Charleston. The Confederates fired upon the fort for more than thirty hours, inflicting

The first battle of the Civil War took place at Fort Sumter on April 12–13, 1861.

heavy damage, until the Union forces finally gave up. No soldier on either side was killed during the bombardment. Meanwhile, Lincoln called for volunteers to fight against the rebellion and ordered the navy to blockade Southern ports.

To protect the harbor, South Carolinians built a series of forts equipped with heavy guns. They also put mines and torpedo boats in the water. These defenses protected Charleston for most of the war.

In May 1862, a black sailor named Robert Smalls was able to pilot a Confederate steamer out of the harbor and give it to the Union fleet, which was blocking the coast and keeping supplies away. The information he gave Union officers about Charleston's defenses helped them launch an attack. But the attack failed.

GLORY

Glory, a 1989 movie starring Matthew Broderick as a Union commander and Denzel Washington as an escaped slave, tells the dramatic story of the Fifty-fourth Massachusetts Regiment. The film won three Academy Awards.

In July 1863, Union forces launched an attack on Charleston Harbor spearheaded by the Fifty-fourth Massachusetts Regiment, made up of freed black slaves. This Union attack was also unsuccessful. But Charleston was weakened by the Union blockade and years of bombardment, and Confederate troops abandoned the city in February 1865, leaving it defenseless.

In early 1865, Union troops under the command of General William T. Sherman burned the city of Columbia and cut a wide path of destruction as they marched through the state. The largest Confederate army, located in Virginia, surrendered to Union forces on April 9, 1865. Fighting ended everywhere over the following weeks. After four years of bloody fighting, the South was defeated, and the Civil War was over.

Recovering from the War

For South Carolina, the Civil War changed everything. The Emancipation Proclamation, signed by President Lincoln on January 1, 1863, essentially freed all slaves in the state (some 400,000 as of the 1860 U.S. census). Those that had not already escaped were freed as territory fell into Union hands. At the end of 1865, the Thirteenth Amendment to the U.S. Constitution officially abolished slavery throughout the United States. Slavery in South Carolina was over.

At the same time, more than 20,000 South Carolinian soldiers died during the war. The economy ended up in ruins, and resources were few. The state had a long hard road of rebuilding ahead.

Right after the war, white leaders who did not want the South to change governed South Carolina. They passed laws that restricted the rights of former

Fort Moultrie is part of Fort Sumter National Monument. It has been used as a military base in conflicts from the American Revolution to World War II.

slaves and forced them, in effect, to continue working on plantations. By 1867, however, the federal government had taken a more active role in managing the states that had formed the Confederacy.

During what became known as the period of Reconstruction, the U.S. Congress appointed military commanders to take control. The federal government required Southern states to pass new constitutions that kept former Confederate leaders from governing and gave former slaves the right to vote.

On June 25, 1868, South Carolina was readmitted to the Union. Under Reconstruction, African Americans began to gain rights as free Americans. Some were even elected to public office. Many black children were able to attend school for the first time.

These measures angered many white people. Some of them resorted to violence. Some whites joined a secret society known as the Ku Klux Klan. Dressed in white robes or sheets, they burned crosses to frighten those who opposed them. They attacked both black and white public officials to drive them out of the new government. They used violence to intimidate and prevent black residents from voting. In what was known as lynching, black people who angered white

This photograph from about 1905 shows Benjamin Tillman, who served as South Carolina's governor from 1890 to 1894.

people or were considered guilty of a crime might be carried off and executed, often by hanging.

In April 1877, federal troops were removed from South Carolina. Wade Hampton, a wealthy plantation owner, became governor, and Reconstruction ended. African Americans soon began to lose the rights they had won, especially after Benjamin Tillman became governor in 1890. Tillman promoted programs to help poor farmers, but he also believed in "white supremacy." He got the state constitution rewritten to limit voting rights for African Americans and require by law that black students attend separate schools from those attended by white children.

So-called Jim Crow laws were also passed to require segregation—separation of whites and blacks—on trains and buses, in restaurants, and in other public facilities. These laws remained in effect until Congress passed the Civil Rights Act of 1964, which outlawed discrimination in public places and in the workplace.

In another way, South Carolina did make a recovery from the effects of the Civil War. In time, the state's economy began to improve. The ports hummed with activity. Farmers were able to sell their crops. Cotton textile mills were built throughout the upcountry. They were highly profitable and provided many jobs.

Not everyone profited, however. Work in the mills was mainly for white people. Families often had trouble making ends meet, and young children were sent to work in mills and factories. The hours were long, the pay was low, and

During the Reconstruction era, the Ku Klux Klan terrorized African Americans and their white supporters. Members of a revival group gather for a rally in 1965.

workers, especially children, were often injured on the job or became ill as a result of poor working conditions. Labor laws establishing a minimum work age and improving some working conditions were eventually passed in the late 1930s.

Ups and Downs

When the Great Depression hit the United States in the 1930s, many South Carolinians lost their jobs and homes. The prices farmers received for their crops fell sharply. Many people left the state in search of better opportunities. African Americans, who had already been suffering from discrimination and a lack of opportunities, were especially hard hit. Increasing numbers of black people moved to northern cities, including New York, Chicago, and Detroit.

Under federal government programs, workers were given jobs building roads, dams, and other projects. Slowly the economy began to recover.

World War II (1939–1945) also helped the economy. South Carolina workers went back to the factories and farms to provide the supplies needed on the battlefront. Military bases opened up near Charleston, providing other jobs. After the United States entered the war in 1941, many South Carolinians served in the armed forces.

During the twentieth century, South Carolina reduced its reliance on a few big crops and developed tourism and other industries to help grow the economy. The economy suffered again in the recession, or economic downturn, that hit the nation and world starting in late 2007. But South Carolinians remained hopeful that, in the long run, the state would continue its economic progress.

During the 1950s and 1960s, for the first time since the end of Reconstruction, the state's African Americans began to see progress. In the early 1950s, a state poll tax that prevented many black people from voting was eliminated. Measures were also taken to curb the Ku Klux Klan, which had revived in the 1920s.

Many white people in South Carolina remained opposed to ending segregation in schools. South Carolina's Strom Thurmond ran for president in

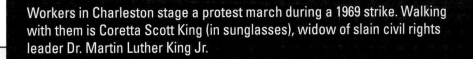

Workers in Charleston stage a protest march during a 1969 strike. Walking with them is Coretta Scott King (in sunglasses), widow of slain civil rights leader Dr. Martin Luther King Jr.

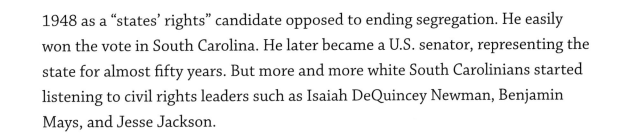

1948 as a "states' rights" candidate opposed to ending segregation. He easily won the vote in South Carolina. He later became a U.S. senator, representing the state for almost fifty years. But more and more white South Carolinians started listening to civil rights leaders such as Isaiah DeQuincey Newman, Benjamin Mays, and Jesse Jackson.

Changing Times

South Carolina's first chapters of the National Association for the Advancement of Colored People (NAACP) had been set up in 1917. With the civil rights movement gaining momentum in the 1950s, the NAACP attracted more members and became a stronger political voice. Sit-ins, marches, and demonstrations were organized to oppose segregation and discrimination against African Americans. The South Carolina tune "We Shall Overcome" became the movement's anthem. The many black people who had before been voiceless now held the power to seek justice.

The 1954 Supreme Court decision barring segregation in public education met with resistance in the state. However, by the end of the 1960s, the state's public schools were all integrated. Black students and white students no longer had to attend separate schools.

Racial tensions did not go away. In 1962, for example, the legislature voted to fly the Confederate flag from the top of the statehouse in Columbia. The flag had different meanings for different people. For many African Americans and others, it stood for a long history of enslavement and oppression of black people. The NAACP protested and started a boycott of the state's tourism industry. Many companies dropped plans to hold conventions in the state. In 2000, the legislature did vote to remove the flag. At the same time, lawmakers agreed to have a smaller version of the flag fly on top of a nearby monument to fallen Confederate soldiers.

Some believed the legislature had gone too far by removing the flag. Others thought it had not gone far enough, and the NAACP continued its boycott. However, most South Carolinians now agree that people of all races and ethnic backgrounds should be able to live in harmony.

In a positive sign of progress, Nikki Haley, a South Carolina state legislator and a daughter of immigrants from India, was elected governor in 2010. She became the first member of a racial minority and the first woman to serve as the state's chief executive.

★ **1526** Lucas Vásquez de Ayllón founds San Miguel de Gualdape, the first European settlement on what is now U.S. soil.

★ **1670** English settlers establish the first permanent European settlement in what is now South Carolina. After being moved nearby, it grows into the city of Charleston.

★ **1715** The Yamassee War breaks out between American Indians and white settlers.

★ **1776** Early in the American Revolution, British forces attack what became Charleston and are beaten back at Sullivan's Island.

★ **1780** The British capture today's Charleston. Patriot farmers win a victory in the Battle of Kings Mountain.

★ **1788** South Carolina becomes the eighth state to ratify the U.S. Constitution.

★ **1860** South Carolina is the first state to secede from the Union.

★ **1861** Confederate troops fire on Fort Sumter, starting off the Civil War.

★ **1868** South Carolina is readmitted to the Union.

★ **1877** Reconstruction ends.

★ **1895** A new state constitution, championed by Governor Benjamin Tillman, in effect ends voting rights for African Americans.

★ **1963** African Americans are admitted to previously all-white public schools in South Carolina.

★ **1970** South Carolina gets its first African-American lawmakers since 1902.

★ **1989** Hurricane Hugo causes billions of dollars in damage in South Carolina.

★ **1995** The Citadel military academy in Charleston admits its first female student.

★ **2000** The Confederate flag is removed from the statehouse.

★ **2003** Strom Thurmond retires after serving almost fifty years in the U.S. Senate.

★ **2010** Nikki Haley, a daughter of Asian immigrants, becomes the first member of a racial minority and the first woman to be elected governor of South Carolina.

3

The People

South Carolina has a smaller proportion of foreign-born residents than most other states. In all, about 96 percent of the state's residents today were born in the United States. Three out of every four people who live in South Carolina were born there. Many claim that their ancestors were among those who settled South Carolina centuries ago.

In its early days, South Carolina was a state of plantations and small farms. Today, three out of five people in South Carolina live in urban areas. Columbia, the capital, is the biggest city. Other cities include Charleston, North Charleston, Rock Hill, Mount Pleasant, Greenville, Summerville, Spartanburg, and Sumter.

About two-thirds of South Carolina's people are white. Most of the rest are African

A vacationer steers a remote-control boat at Myrtle Beach.

A mother and daughter enjoy the South Carolina seashore.

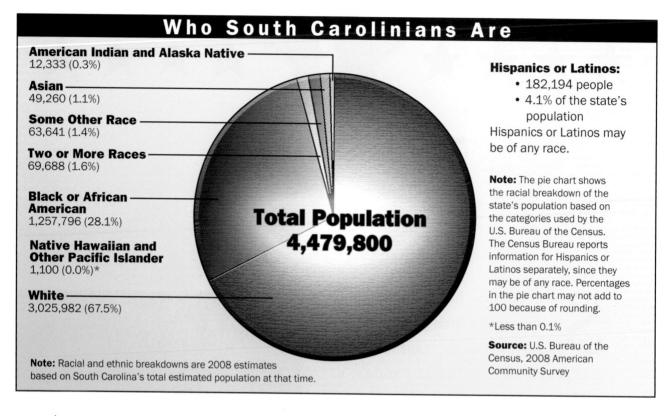

American Indian and Alaska Native
12,333 (0.3%)

Asian
49,260 (1.1%)

Some Other Race
63,641 (1.4%)

Two or More Races
69,688 (1.6%)

Black or African American
1,257,796 (28.1%)

Native Hawaiian and Other Pacific Islander
1,100 (0.0%)*

White
3,025,982 (67.5%)

Total Population
4,479,800

Hispanics or Latinos:
- 182,194 people
- 4.1% of the state's population

Hispanics or Latinos may be of any race.

Note: The pie chart shows the racial breakdown of the state's population based on the categories used by the U.S. Bureau of the Census. The Census Bureau reports information for Hispanics or Latinos separately, since they may be of any race. Percentages in the pie chart may not add to 100 because of rounding.

*Less than 0.1%

Source: U.S. Bureau of the Census, 2008 American Community Survey

Note: Racial and ethnic breakdowns are 2008 estimates based on South Carolina's total estimated population at that time.

American. There are small numbers of American Indians and Asian Americans. Hispanics, or Latinos, make up about 4 percent of the total state population.

American Indians in South Carolina

Long before Europeans settled in the region, American Indians were hunting and farming on the land. They had developed their own governments, social structures, and traditions. As European explorers and settlers arrived, the Indian population declined sharply. Indian tribes also often lost their homelands. In the late 1830s, members of the powerful Cherokee people were forced by the U.S. government to leave South Carolina and other southeastern states and march about 1,000 miles (1,600 km) to Oklahoma. About one in four died on the brutal journey, in what is called the Trail of Tears.

Another tribe was pressured by the state into selling its land for new territory in North Carolina. This tribe, the Catawba Indians, never received that land, but they did acquire a smaller reservation in South Carolina. In 1993, they were

Cherokee and Catawba Indians join in a powwow.

awarded $50 million by the federal government in return for dropping their land claims. Today, there are a few thousand Catawba Indians in South Carolina. Many live near Rock Hill, close to their original territory along the banks of the Catawba River.

In all, there are about 12,000 American Indians in South Carolina. Many have tried to preserve their culture and share it with others. For example, the Day of the Catawba is an annual event held on the Saturday after Thanksgiving. It includes dance demonstrations, traditional music, and displays of Catawba pottery.

MAKING A DANCE RATTLE

The Catawba Indians of South Carolina have many lively storytelling and dance traditions. In one event, called the Stomp Dance, women wear rattles, made from turtle shells, wrapped around their legs. In other events, men dance, chant, beat drums, and shake rattles made of turtle shells, cow horns, or rawhide. The rattles are filled with beans or small stones. See if you can make your own Catawba rattle.

WHAT YOU NEED

2 very thin pieces of rawhide (dog chews from the grocery store work well) or a piece of cardboard about $8\frac{1}{2}$ by 11 inches (22 by 28 cm)

Pen

Scissors

Hole puncher

Unsharpened wooden pencil

Masking tape

Glue

3 or 4 small feathers (such as those in a feather duster or a dress-up feather boa)

1 piece of brown fabric (fake suede or velveteen fabric works well) about 4 by 20 inches (10 by 50 cm)

A handful of dried beans, corn, peas, or very small stones

1 piece of yarn or cord about 10 to 12 inches (25 to 30 cm) long

6 to 12 colored beads

On the piece of cardboard or the two pieces of rawhide, draw two circles with a pen. The diameter, or width, of each circle should be about 3 inches (8 cm). You can use the bottom of a jar or glass to trace an even circle. Then, using the scissors, cut out the circles. If you are working with rawhide, you may find it difficult to cut the circles (the rawhide may be tough). Ask an adult to help you if necessary.

Using the hole puncher, make holes around the entire edge of one circle, keeping them about 1/2 to 3/4 inch (1 to 2 cm) apart. Punching the holes can be tough, so ask an adult to help.

After making holes in the first piece, punch holes in the second piece. Make sure to line up the holes with those in the first piece.

Line up the two pieces and place the pencil between them, making sure that only one end of the handle sticks out. Tape the pencil to the inside of one of the pieces, in between the punched-out holes. Glue feathers in place near the edges of the pieces.

Then, cut a strip of fabric about 1/2 by 20 inches (1 by 50 cm). Tie the two pieces of rawhide or cardboard together by weaving the fabric strip through each of the holes. Before lacing through the last hole, slip the beans, peas, or rocks in between the pieces. Finish lacing and knot the ends of the fabric together tightly.

Cut a piece of fabric about 1 by 20 inches (2.5 by 50 cm) and wrap it around the pencil. Glue the ends of the fabric to make them stick to the pencil. Cut the piece of yarn or cord in half. On each half, tie a knot at one end and thread on a few beads. Tie each piece of yarn or cord to the rattle through one of the punched holes, letting the pieces of yarn dangle. Now you are ready to shake your rattle.

Quick Facts

HUMBLE BEGINNINGS

Andrew Jackson, the seventh U.S. president, was born in a backwoods cabin near the border between North Carolina and South Carolina. His parents were Scots-Irish immigrants. He grew up poor and had little education.

Settlers from Europe

Wealthy English colonists from Barbados settled the city of Charleston (then Charles Towne) in 1670. They built large plantations and used slaves to work the land. They were joined by other settlers from the British Isles, including Irish from Northern Ireland and Scots-Irish and others from Scotland. Some of the early settlers were Protestants who did not belong to the Church of England. They were often discriminated against at home.

In the colony's early days, Scottish immigrants were not allowed to hold office. Eventually, Scottish men and women went on to become governors, members of Congress, and state legislators in the state. These days, Scottish cultural celebrations called ceilidhs (pronounced KAY-lays) are held in towns across South Carolina from Sumter to Aiken.

Descendants of the early English, Scottish, and Irish settlers, and of immigrants from the British Isles who arrived and settled in this part of the country over the years, make up the largest single group of white people living in South Carolina today.

People of German origin have been farming in the Orangeburg and Amelia regions since the early 1600s. Their farming practices helped them produce so much wheat that the area became known as the Breadbasket of South Carolina. Today, about one in ten South Carolinians is of German descent.

Another group of South Carolinians is of French origin. South Carolina had the largest French population of any of the original thirteen colonies. Many of these settlers were French Protestants known as Huguenots. They suffered persecution in Catholic France but had religious freedom in South Carolina. They found work as carpenters, cobblers, tailors, and craftsmen and held seats in the legislature. Their descendants can be found in different parts of the state today.

A LONG TRADITION

Charleston is the home of the nation's oldest Jewish synagogue building in continuous use— and the second-oldest synagogue building in the United States. Sephardic Jews who had been expelled from Spain and Portugal founded Kahal Kadosh Beth Elohim synagogue in 1749. In its early days, Charleston became known as the Holy City because it had so many religious sites.

Francis Marion: Military Leader

Born in the colony of South Carolina around 1732, Francis Marion became a military hero in the American Revolution. He is best known for leading his small group of poorly equipped men in raids against British troops and Loyalist Americans who supported the British. He earned the nickname the "Swamp Fox" because he and his men often struck at night and then disappeared into the swamps and marshes. He died in 1795.

John C. Calhoun: Politician

Born near Abbeville, South Carolina, in 1782, John C. Calhoun was one of the most important political figures of the state. During his long career, he served as a U.S. representative, senator, secretary of war, and secretary of state. He also served as vice president under two presidents. Seeking to protect slavery and other Southern interests, he argued that states could disregard federal laws that they thought violated their rights. He died in 1850, eleven years before the Civil War.

Mary McLeod Bethune: Educator and Activist

Mary McLeod Bethune was born in 1875 in Mayesville, to parents who had been slaves. She believed education was the key to success, and taught in several different schools that struggled to survive. In 1904, she opened a training school in Florida for African-American girls that became Bethune-Cookman College. Bethune worked actively for the advancement of African Americans and was an adviser to three presidents. She died in 1955.

Dizzy Gillespie: Musician

Dizzy (John Birks) Gillespie was born in 1917 in Cheraw. A well-respected trombone and trumpet player, he revolutionized jazz music with his energetic, fast-paced style called bebop. In 1975, he won a Grammy, and in 1989, he was awarded the National Medal of Arts. Gillespie died in 1993.

Althea Gibson: Athlete

Althea Gibson was born in 1927 in Silver, South Carolina. Sometimes called the Jackie Robinson of tennis, she was the first black woman to win Grand Slam championships, in the 1950s. Among many victories, she won the women's singles title two times each at Wimbledon and at the U.S. Open. In 1957, she was the first African American to be voted Female Athlete of the Year by the Associated Press. She died in 2003.

Nikki Haley: Politician

Nikki Haley was born in 1972 in Bamberg. Her parents were immigrants from India. They built up a highly successful clothing company, which she later helped run. Elected in 2004 to the state house of representatives, she was the first Indian American to win public office in the state. In 2010, she was elected the 116th governor of the state.

Basket weaving is one of many traditions that the Gullahs have passed from generation to generation.

African Americans in South Carolina

Close to one-third of all South Carolinians are African American, and many are descended from enslaved people. Slaves who worked on the islands off South Carolina's eastern coast had little contact with their owners, who lived mostly on the mainland while overseers ran the plantation. Left to themselves, the slaves developed and preserved a culture based on African traditions. These people were called the Gullahs.

At the start of the Civil War, Union troops occupied the Sea Islands, freeing the slaves there. Most chose to remain on the islands, farming the land for northern investors. The Gullahs continued to live and work there. To this day, they keep alive their fishing, weaving, storytelling, and music traditions. From bells and rattles to xylophones and one-string fiddles, Gullah music is full of traditional rhythms and styles.

The growth of tourism and the development of luxury resorts have put pressure on the Gullah way of life. With the help of such organizations as the Sea Islands Preservation Project, the Gullahs are working to protect their land and culture and encourage balanced development.

Other African Americans in the state are descended from slaves who were brought to the South Carolina mainland. Some come from immigrant families who left Africa or other parts of the world later on, or from families that moved into the state from different parts of the country. Regardless of their origins, African Americans are a vital part of South Carolina communities and businesses.

Hispanic Americans and Asian Americans

Though many South Carolinians have roots in the state that go back for generations, newcomers have contributed to the state's growth in recent decades. They come from all parts of the world, including from Asia and from Mexico and Spanish-speaking countries or areas in Central America, South America, and the Caribbean.

The Hispanic, or Latino, population in South Carolina is fairly small, but it has been growing. Some Hispanics are migrant workers who come to the United States—perhaps temporarily and sometimes without having obtained permission to enter the country—to earn money to send back home. They often work very hard harvesting crops for low pay. Outreach groups and special programs have been set up

South Carolina is home to a growing Hispanic population.

Two swimmers play at Lake Hartwell in the foothills of the Blue Ridge Mountains.

to help these migrant workers and their families. Other Latinos are American citizens who have moved recently from Spanish-speaking countries or lived in South Carolina for years. Hispanics are an active and important part of the state's industries, government, and educational system.

The Asian-American population in South Carolina is small, but immigrants continue to move to the state from countries such as China, Japan, South Korea, the Philippines, and India. Some Asian communities hold traditional celebrations during the year. Restaurants and stores specializing in Asian food and other products are becoming more common in different parts of the state.

Why South Carolina?

People live in South Carolina for many reasons. The state's mild climate is an attraction, along with its sunny beaches, scenic countryside, and historical heritage. Some find work in cities such as Charleston, Columbia, Greenville, Sumter, and Myrtle Beach and settle there or in nearby suburbs. Others live on farms that have been in their families for generations. The coastal and island communities are popular places to live as well as to visit. Many Americans from other parts of the country move there when they retire. As people continue to move to South Carolina, their cultures, traditions, and fresh ideas contribute to the state's growth and prosperity.

Cadets march in full-dress uniform at The Citadel, the highly respected military college in Charleston.

★ Lowcountry Oyster Festival

The World's Biggest Oyster Festival is held in January at the Boone Hall Plantation in Mount Pleasant. It offers plenty of food, an oyster-eating contest, and a kids' corner with pony rides and a jumpy castle.

★ Governor's Annual Frog Jumping Contest

Every year on the day before Easter, Springfield hosts this fun event. The winning frog goes on to California to compete with jumping frogs from all over the country.

★ World Grits Festival

This festival, held each April in St. George, includes a Rolling-in-the-Grits contest, as well as grits grinding demonstrations, gospel music, and a parade.

★ A Taste of Beaufort

This event, held in late April or early May, features lowcountry food, live music, and activities for children.

★ Gullah Cultural Festival

The Gullah Festival, held in Beaufort in late May, celebrates the culture of the enslaved Africans who worked and lived on the coastal plantations. Along with music and food, there are demonstrations of storytelling, basket weaving, and other Gullah skills that have been preserved.

★ Spoleto Festival USA

For about two weeks starting around Memorial Day, Charleston's theaters, churches, and outdoor spaces offer more than a hundred theater, music, dance, and opera performances by artists from around the world.

★ Watermelon Festival

This festival, held in Hampton County in June, is one of the oldest in South Carolina. The first celebration was held in 1939. It offers parades, contests, music, and lots of watermelon.

★ Carolina Day

On June 28, South Carolinians celebrate the 1776 American victory at the Battle of Fort Moultrie. At the fort itself, on Sullivan's Island, families can enjoy musket and artillery demonstrations, a children's program, and a band concert.

★ Scottish Games and Highland Gathering

These events are held in September at the Boone Hall Plantation in Mount Pleasant—and at other sites in several states and Scotland itself. Visitors can enjoy Highland fling and Scottish country dancing, pipers, fiddlers, and traditional Scottish sports.

★ MOJA Arts Festival

Moja is a Swahili word for "one." The MOJA festival is a celebration of the many African-American and Caribbean traditions still alive in Charleston. The festival, held around late September and early October, spotlights African forms of theater, dance, and visual art.

★ State Fair

Dating from 1869, the state fair is held in Columbia each year in October. There are farm animal competitions, displays of student art, and carnival rides.

How the Government Works

The Charleston city government operates in this building, which dates back to 1804.

Running a state requires a lot of hard work from many people. At the local level, towns and cities have their own governments. They handle matters that affect the town or city, such as zoning and police and fire protection. On the next level are the state's forty-six county governments. They handle matters that affect the county as a whole.

State Government

The state government deals with issues relating to the whole state. Like the federal government, it is made up of three branches: the executive, the legislative, and the judicial. Each branch has its own responsibilities.

Columbia is the state capital. Near the center of South Carolina, it is the

Lawmakers meet in the South Carolina State House in Columbia.

The inside of the South Carolina State House was renovated in the 1990s.

city where most state officials work and the legislature meets. The governor's mansion is located there.

The state government of South Carolina spends more than $20 billion a year. More than 40 percent of the money is used for health care and social services, and about 35 percent is spent on education.

Where does the state get its money? About 60 percent of it comes from state taxes and fees. These include the sales taxes on items that people buy and the state income taxes that citizens and companies must pay depending on how much money they earn. The rest of the state's money comes from the federal government.

How a Bill Becomes a Law

When the general assembly is meeting, any member of the senate or house of representatives can propose a new law and try to get it passed. A proposed law is called a bill. A bill introduced by a senator is first considered in the senate, and a bill proposed by a representative is first considered in the house. The bill

Branches of Government

EXECUTIVE ★ ★ ★ ★ ★ ★ ★ ★

The governor supervises the state government, plans the budget, appoints certain officials, and approves or rejects bills that are passed by the legislature. He or she serves a four-year term and cannot serve more than two terms in a row. The lieutenant governor, secretary of state, and attorney general also serve four-year terms.

LEGISLATIVE ★ ★ ★ ★ ★ ★ ★ ★

Members of this branch belong to the state legislature, which is called the general assembly. They make the state's laws and must approve a state budget each year. The general assembly is divided into two houses, or chambers. The upper house, or senate, has 46 members elected to four-year terms. The lower house, or house of representatives, has 124 members, elected to two-year terms. There is no limit on the number of terms that legislators may serve.

JUDICIAL ★ ★ ★ ★ ★ ★ ★ ★

The supreme court is the highest court in the state. Its five justices are elected by the general assembly and serve ten-year terms. The supreme court reviews decisions made by lower-level state courts and can decide whether or not a state law agrees with the state constitution. Beneath the supreme court is the court of appeals, with ten judges elected to six-year terms. The court of appeals can review decisions made by circuit courts and other lower courts that hold trials.

is read out loud and then sent to a committee of lawmakers. Their job is to examine the bill carefully, perhaps make changes to it, and then accept or reject it. If a majority of the committee votes to accept the bill, it goes to the full chamber for consideration, possible further changes, and then a vote.

If a majority of the members of one chamber vote to accept a version of the bill, it is sent to the other house, where the process of considering and voting on the bill is repeated. The second chamber may make changes to the bill it received before passing it. In that case, the bill usually goes to a special committee (called a conference committee), made up of members from each house, who agree on a final version of the bill. This final version must then be passed again by both houses.

When both houses have passed the bill in exactly the same form, it goes to the governor. The governor can accept and sign the bill, in which case it becomes a law. The bill also becomes a law if the governor takes no action on it for five days. The governor may also reject (veto) the bill. In order for a vetoed bill to become a law, two-thirds of the members in each house must then vote for it.

What You Can Do

When you get to the age of eighteen, you will be able to vote. In the meantime, it is a good idea to learn about what is going on in your state. Newspapers and

Local college football players volunteer to celebrate reading with children in a Richland County Public Library program.

television news programs can help you understand important issues and learn more about the people who represent you. You can also contact these representatives about issues that concern you.

There are also other ways to make a difference in your community. In South Carolina, as in other states, children and adults can volunteer in their communities. You may be able to help out at a local religious organization, animal shelter, food kitchen, or home for the elderly.

One of the shining stars of South Carolina's volunteer programs is PalmettoPride. This nonprofit organization has won awards for its work keeping the Palmetto State clean by promoting recycling and the reduction of litter. The organization's website offers kid-friendly activities and details about joining or setting up a litter initiative.

Contacting Lawmakers

★ ★ ★ ★ ★ ★ ★ ★ ★ ★ ★

To find out who your legislators in South Carolina are and how to contact them, go to

http://www.scstatehouse.gov

Click on "Find Your Legislator" on the left side. Then click on "Find Your 9-digit Zip Code," unless you know it already. You will be asked to type your address in order to get it. Once you have your 9-digit zip code, you can type it into the boxes shown.

You will get to a screen that lists your representatives in both the state and the federal government. Click on a name to get contact information.

Quick Facts

REPRESENTATIVES IN CONGRESS

Voters in South Carolina elect lawmakers to represent them in the U.S. Congress in Washington, D.C. Like all other states, South Carolina has two U.S. senators. The number of members a state can elect to the U.S. House of Representatives is based on its population in the latest census. After the 2010 Census, South Carolina was entitled to seven seats in the House of Representatives.

Making a Living

South Carolinians make a living in many different ways. Some work as farmers or fishers, and many more work in factories or in the construction industry. But the largest number of workers, by far, provide services to other people or businesses instead of producing a product. The service industry includes people working in education, health care, wholesale or retail business, media, entertainment, and the government, among other fields. Many service workers in South Carolina have jobs at one of the military bases in the state. Others work at the docks in Charleston, where cargo ships from all over the world load and unload.

Tourism

About 30 million people visit South Carolina each year. Visitors flock to the resorts along the coast every summer. In addition, the many state parks and Congaree National Park provide opportunities for hiking, biking, canoeing, and camping. The state's lakes, rivers, and streams draw boaters and fishers throughout the year.

People also come to South Carolina to enjoy its historic beauty. Since South Carolina was one of the thirteen original colonies, it has a long and rich history. Historic buildings, plantations, battlefields, and other sites are open to the public. South Carolina offers many ways to learn about the history of

An assembly-line worker builds
a luxury car in a Greer auto plant.

Workers & Industries

Industry	Number of People Working in That Industry	Percentage of All Workers Who Are Working in That Industry
Education and health care	419,315	20.8%
Manufacturing	292,586	14.5%
Wholesale and retail businesses	289,439	14.3%
Publishing, media, entertainment, hotels, and restaurants	239,382	11.8%
Professionals, scientists, and managers	175,096	8.7%
Construction	167,492	8.3%
Banking and finance, insurance, and real estate	124,214	6.1%
Transportation and public utilities	99,801	4.9%
Other services	98,816	4.9%
Government	96,272	4.8%
Farming, fishing, forestry, and mining	17,813	0.9%
Totals	2,020,226	100%

Notes: Figures above do not include people in the armed forces. "Professionals" includes people such as doctors and lawyers. Percentages may not add to 100 because of rounding.

Source: U.S. Bureau of the Census, 2008 estimates

Myrtle Beach State Park is a fun place for South Carolinians and out-of-state visitors alike.

the state as well as the country. South Carolina is also home to many museums and theaters.

During the tourist season, thousands of workers are hired at beachfront hotels, state parks, restaurants, water parks, and other facilities. The money that tourists spend in South Carolina creates one out of every ten of the state's jobs. The state also relies on various taxes to fund state and local governments. South Carolinians pay income taxes on the money they earn, and everyone—including tourists—pays sales tax on purchases in the state.

RECIPE FOR SOUTH CAROLINA BARBECUE SAUCE

The Carolinas are known for their (non-tomato) barbecue sauces. Here is one recipe for a barbecue sauce with a mustard and vinegar base.

WHAT YOU NEED

$1/4$ teaspoon (1 milliliter) cayenne pepper

1 teaspoon (5 ml) black pepper

1 tablespoon (15 ml) chili powder

$1/2$ cup (100 grams) regular white sugar, packed firmly

$1/4$ cup (50 g) light brown sugar, packed firmly

$2/3$ cup (150 ml) yellow mustard

3 drops of Tabasco sauce

1 cup (250 ml) cider vinegar

$1/2$ teaspoon (3 ml) soy sauce

2 tablespoons (30 g) butter

In a mixing bowl, combine the peppers, chili powder, and sugars. Add the mustard and Tabasco sauce. Add the vinegar into the bowl and mix well.

Pour the mixture into a small pot. Let the sauce simmer on the stove for at least 10 minutes. Be sure to ask an adult to help you with the stove. As the sauce simmers, stir in the soy sauce and butter. Continue stirring for 5 to 10 minutes. Take the pot off of the stove, and your sauce is ready.

Many South Carolinians use barbecue sauce on pork, beef, and chicken. (If you plan on preparing the meat yourself, have an adult help you to make sure the meat is fully cooked.) You can coat the cooked meat with the sauce or use the sauce on the side for dipping. If the sauce is too spicy—or not spicy enough—adjust the amounts of chili powder and Tabasco sauce to suit your taste.

Cotton fields grow on the Boone Hall Plantation grounds in Charleston.

Farming and Fishing

Field crops such as cotton were once the biggest moneymakers for South Carolina. Although agriculture is much less important now, it remains a vital part of the economy. The chief sources of farm income today include chickens, greenhouse and nursery products, turkeys, cattle, and dairy products. South Carolina farmers also grow corn, soybeans, wheat, tobacco, hay, watermelons, apples, peanuts, and pecans. Cotton is still grown in some counties. The Palmetto State also produces more peaches than any other state except California.

Seafood is a popular South Carolina product. Shrimp, crabs, oysters, and clams are harvested on the coast. Ocean fish are also important. Fresh seafood is served in restaurants throughout the state. It is also shipped to other states.

Manufacturing

Manufacturing now brings in about one-sixth of the state's income. Leading products include automobiles and other transportation equipment. Textile manufacturing has declined but remains important. South Carolina's factories turn out cotton, silk, wool, polyester, acrylics, and nylon. Some factories make the fabric into clothes.

South Carolina also has a productive chemical industry. Factories across the state manufacture chemicals for fertilizers used on farms in South Carolina and other states. In addition to manufacturing useful products, the factories provide jobs for South Carolinians.

WE "FINISH" ON TIME

2,8,3 DAYS SINCE THE LAST LATE ORDER

South Carolina factories manufacture a variety of products, including textiles.

Marine recruits drill at Parris Island. This federal military base is part of South Carolina's economy.

The federal government also brings money into the state. There are several military bases in South Carolina. The Savannah River Site removes nuclear material from decommissioned weapons and serves as a nuclear storage facility. The Department of Defense also uses this site for other nuclear research.

Like other states, South Carolina has lost many manufacturing jobs in recent years. The state is relying more and more on job growth in other parts of the economy to help create opportunities for workers in the years ahead.

Golf

People from all over the United States travel to South Carolina to play golf. The state's landscape and its warm weather make it a perfect home for golf courses. Each year close to 2 million rounds of golf are played in the Myrtle Beach area.

Poultry

Farmers in many parts of the state produce poultry products, including eggs, chickens, and turkeys. Most of South Carolina's livestock income comes from poultry farms.

Historic Plantations

Many of the sprawling plantations that once flourished in South Carolina have been preserved and renovated. They are open to visitors interested in learning about life in the South before the Civil War.

Trees

Trees cover about two-thirds of the state and contribute to South Carolina's beauty. Some trees are grown to be shipped to other states for landscaping and gardening. At the same time, timber from trees is the state's most important crop. The timber industry provides jobs for more than 30,000 South Carolinians.

Industrial Machinery

Making special machines, equipment, and parts for use in factories and warehouses is one of the state's biggest industries. Jobs in this sector have increased, while the textile industry and other manufacturing industries have lost jobs in recent years.

Peaches

Among the fifty states, South Carolina ranks second in overall peach production. The South Carolina Peach Festival is held every July in Gaffney. The town also has a water tower that is designed to look like a huge peach.

Businesses large and small have grown along with the population in South Carolina.

Finding the Right Balance

South Carolina has to balance the need for jobs and economic growth with the need to protect the natural resources of the land. Over the past few decades, as the population has grown, more land has been developed to make room for houses, roadways, and shopping centers. Heavy development in parts of the Sea Islands has crowded out natural habitats for egrets, alligators, and rare bird species. Also of concern to many is the storage of nuclear wastes at the Savannah River Site, not far from major cities in South Carolina and Georgia.

In 1989, the South Carolina Environmental Excellence Program (SCEEP) was set up. Companies and organizations that join this program agree to try to improve the environment by preventing pollution and conserving energy and other resources.

In order to create jobs, businesses need to grow. At the same time, it is up to everybody to care for and respect the land.

The state flag of South Carolina was adopted in 1861. It is blue with a palmetto tree and a silver crescent. Blue is the color of the uniforms worn by the soldiers who fought in the American Revolution. The crescent looks like the symbol on the soldiers' hats. The palmetto tree represents the colonists' victory over the British at Sullivan's Island in 1776.

The left side of the seal has a palmetto tree growing from a fallen oak tree. This represents the defeat of the British at Sullivan's Island. The left side also shows the dates for South Carolina's first constitution (March 26, 1776) and for the Declaration of Independence (July 4, 1776). The right side of the seal shows a woman who symbolizes hope triumphing over danger. The state's two mottos surround the two ovals. On the left are the Latin words Animis Opibusque Parati, meaning "Prepared in Mind and Resources." On the right, Dum Spiro Spero is Latin for "While I Breathe, I Hope."

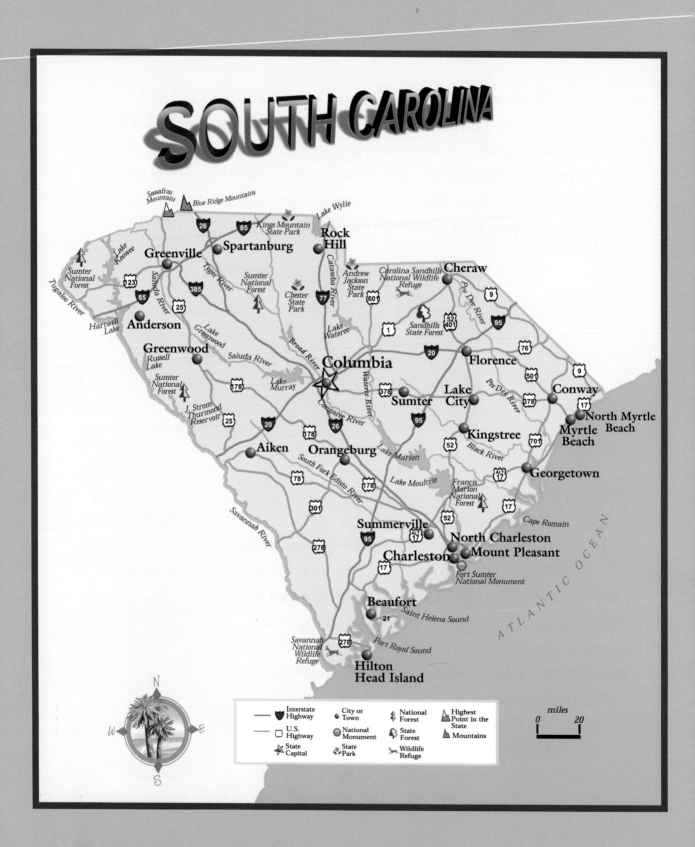

SOUTH CAROLINA

Sassafras Mountain

Blue Ridge Mountains

Lake Wylie

Kings Mountain State Park

Rock Hill

Cheraw

Sumter National Forest

Lake Keowee

Greenville

Spartanburg

Andrew Jackson State Park

Carolina Sandhills National Wildlife Refuge

Pee Dee River

Tiger River

Saluda River

Catawba River

Sumter National Forest

Chester State Park

Lake Wateree

Sandhills State Forest

Tugaloo River

Hartwell Lake

Anderson

Lake Greenwood

Greenwood

Russell Lake

Sumter National Forest

Saluda River

Broad River

Lake Murray

Columbia

Wateree River

Sumter

Lake City

Florence

Pee Dee River

Conway

North Myrtle Beach

J. Strom Thurmond Reservoir

Congaree River

Myrtle Beach

Aiken

Orangeburg

Lake Marion

Kingstree

Black River

South Fork Edisto River

Lake Moultrie

Georgetown

Savannah River

Francis Marion National Forest

Cape Romain

Summerville

North Charleston

Mount Pleasant

Charleston

Fort Sumter National Monument

Beaufort

Saint Helena Sound

A T L A N T I C   O C E A N

Savannah National Wildlife Refuge

Port Royal Sound

Hilton Head Island

Interstate Highway	City or Town	National Forest	Highest Point in the State		
U.S. Highway	National Monument	State Forest	Mountains		
State Capital	State Park	Wildlife Refuge			

miles

0   20

N S E W

Carolina

words by Henry Timrod
music by Anne Custis Burgess

Call on thy child – ren of the hill, Wake swamp and

riv – er, coast and rill, Rouse all thy strength and all thy skill,

Car – o – li – na! Ca – ro – li – na!

BOOKS

Gunderson, Megan M. *Andrew Jackson*. Edina, MN: Abdo Publishing, 2009.

Harmon, Daniel S. *South Carolina: Past and Present*. New York: Rosen Publishing, 2010.

Jerome, Kate Boehm. *Charleston, SC: Cool Stuff Every Kid Should Know*. Mount Pleasant, SC: Arcadia Publishing, 2008.

Kaufman, Scott. *Francis Marion: Swamp Fox of South Carolina*. Stockton, NJ: OTTN Publishing, 2006.

Mis, Melody S. *The Colony of South Carolina: A Primary Source History*. New York: Rosen Publishing, 2006.

WEBSITES

Official South Carolina Site for Kids:
http://sc.gov/facts-history/Pages/KidsPages.aspx

South Carolina Tourism Official Site:
http://www.discoversouthcarolina.com

South Carolina's Information Superhighway:
http://www.sciway.net/hist

Official Website of the State of South Carolina:
http://www.sc.gov

As the editor of *Scholastic News*, **Debra Hess** created educational material for children across America. Ms. Hess has created material for children for Microsoft, written for an award-winning children's television series, and authored dozens of books for children, including *Wilson Sat Alone*, which was made into a PBS Storytime Special, and *Thurgood Marshall: The Fight for Equal Justice*, which was a New York Public Library Best Books for Children.

As editorial director at World Almanac Books, **William McGeveran** helped put together many editions of *The World Almanac and Book of Facts* and *The World Almanac for Kids*. Now a freelance editor and writer, Bill has four grown children and four grandchildren who will soon be old enough to read this book.

INDEX

Page numbers in **boldface** are illustrations.